Elephants

Kate Petty

BARRON'S

The new baby

A baby elephant grows inside its mother for twice as long as a human baby. When the mother elephant is ready to give birth the herd forms a protective circle around her. They make a lot of noise, which keeps other animals away. A female relative helps the mother with the birth. The newborn elephant is just 3 feet tall. It weighs about 220 lbs.

The mother and her helper are safe inside a circle of tusks.

An "auntie" helps the mother with her baby. ▷

Mother and baby

The baby tries to stand only half an hour after it has been born. The "auntie" gently helps it to its feet. The baby reaches up with its mouth to drink milk from its mother's breast. During its first year it will often return to the safe place between its mother's front legs. The baby's first little tusks are called "tushes."

A baby elephant drinks milk from its mother.

The safest place for this African baby elephant ▷

New member

The baby elephant soon finds its feet. After two days the mother and her baby are ready to walk with the herd. The herd slows down to the pace of its newest little member. Male elephants as well as females protect the young from danger, though only the females actually see to the needs of the babies.

Mother and baby join the herd.

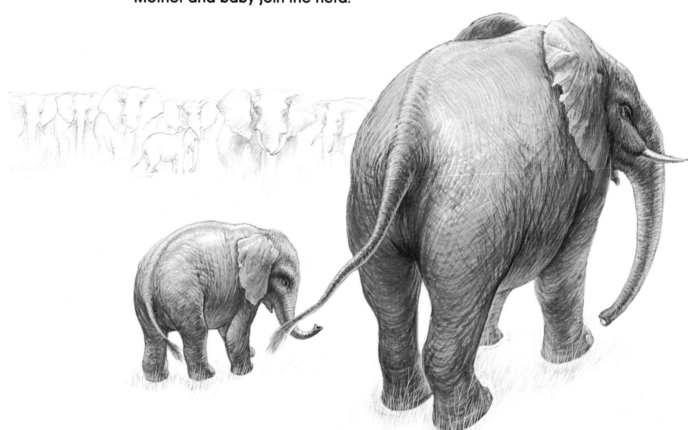

The herd takes a break at a watering hole. ▷

Food and water

A baby elephant drinks milk from its mother for three or four years, sometimes longer. Adult elephants need 330 lbs of food a day and over 26 gallons of water. They eat grass, fruit, bark, twigs, roots and even flowers. Babies learn quite early how to suck up water with their trunks. They squirt it into their mouths to drink or over their heads for a cooling shower.

The baby learns to squirt water with its trunk.

Mother and baby feed at different heights. ▷

The trunk

A baby elephant has to learn to control its trunk as a human baby has to learn to control its legs. The trunk is the elephant's nose. Elephants have a keen sense of smell. The trunk is also like a hand – for feeding and lifting and touching. Its tip is very sensitive. It can act as a wonderful hosepipe for sucking up and spraying water and dust. It makes a good snorkel to breathe through, too, when swimming underwater.

The nostrils are at the sensitive tip of the trunk.

This baby uses its trunk to hold on tight! ▷

Keeping in touch

A mother elephant strokes and guides her baby with her trunk. She catches hold of its tail to keep it from straying. Or she cuffs it when it is naughty. Family members rub against one another in a friendly way. Grazing elephants keep in contact by making low rumbling sounds. Elephants trumpet when they are excited or to frighten other animals away.

Mother and baby touch trunks.

Mother's trunk tells baby the way to go. ▷

Learning and playing

Mother elephants look after their young for 10 years, longer than any other animal except humans. Until it is about two years old a baby elephant depends on its mother for everything and stays close to her. Soon it becomes curious. Little elephants play and explore together in the safety of the family group. They are surrounded by mothers, aunts and older sisters and brothers, who all show them how to behave.

Calves of different ages feed from their mother.

Calves playing together ▷

The family group

Ten or twelve elephants live together in a close family group. The most important is the oldest and strongest female (cow), called the matriarch. Her daughters and their young make up the rest of the family unit. Three or four families make up a herd. The males (bulls) of the herd form their own group and protect the females. If danger threatens, the whole herd bunches together with the weaker ones in the middle.

The matriarch fronts the protective group.

The inquisitive baby will not be allowed to stray far. ▷

Bathtime

Bathtime is very important to the elephant family. Water keeps them cool. You have a bath to wash the mud *off*, but an elephant covers itself in mud *after* a bath! The mudpack protects its skin from insect bites. If there is no water, elephants will cool themselves down with a dust bath instead, using their trunks to spray dust all over themselves.

Elephants obviously enjoy bathing.

This baby Asian elephant loves playing in water. ▷

Growing up

Female elephants never leave their families. If a family group becomes too large, they split up into several smaller groups. Young bulls leave the herd when they are thirteen or fourteen years old. They may live on their own or with other young bulls for a few years. Then they will have to prove their strength before joining a herd.

A bull leaves the elephant herd.

Young bulls sparring for their right to join a herd. ▷

Elephant facts

There are two kinds of elephants, African and Asian. Asian elephants have humped backs and smaller ears than African elephants. Elephants are not weaned until they are two or three years old. The hair they have as babies never disappears – it just looks thinner as they grow bigger. By six years they weigh about 2,200 lbs. They can live independently at 12-14 years.

Index

A
African elephant 22
Asian elephant 19, 22
"auntie" 2

B
bathing 18,19
bull 16, 20

C
communication 12
cow 16

D
drinking 8
dust bath 10, 18

E
eating 8

F
families 12, 14, 16, 20

H
hair 22
herd 2, 6, 7, 16

L
learning 14

M
matriarch 16
milk 4, 8
mud 18

N
newborn 2
noises 12

P
play 14, 15, 16
pregnancy 2
protection 2, 6, 12, 16

S
safety 4, 5, 14, 16
senses 10, 11
size 22
standing 4
suckling 4, 8, 14
swimming 10

T
tail 12
touching 12
trumpeting 12
trunk 8, 10, 12, 13
tusks 2, 4, 21

W
walking 6
watering hole 7
weight 2, 22

Photographic Credits:

Cover and all pages apart from 13 and
21:Bruce Coleman Photo Library; pages 13
and 21:Planet Earth Pictures.

Design   David West Children's
                    Book Design
Illustrations   George Thompson
Picture Research Cee Weston-Baker

First paperback edition for the United Sta
and Canada published 1992 by Barron's
Educational Series, Inc.

First published in the United States 1991 b
Gloucester Press.
© Copyright 1989 by Aladdin Books Ltd

All inquiries should be addressed to:
Barron's Educational Series, Inc.
250 Wireless Boulevard
Hauppauge, New York 11788

Library of Congress
Catalog Card No. 89-26037
International Standard
Book No. 0-8120-4966-7

Library of Congress Cataloging-in-
Publication Data

Petty, Kate.
        Elephants / Kate Petty.
        p. cm.--(Baby animals)
        Includes index.
        Summary: Describes how elephant
are born and cared for and how they lec
to find food and cooperate with their he
   ISBN 0-8120-4966-7 (paperback)
1. Elephants--Infancy--Juvenile Literature.
Elephants--Development--Juvenile
literature. (1. Elephants. 2. Animals--
Infancy.) I. Title. II. Series: Petty, Kate. Bab
animals.
QL737.P98P4   1990
599.6'1--dc20   89-26037
                                 CIP   AC

Printed in Belgium
2345   987654321